T5-CVE-919

CREATIVITY

TAKES FLIGHT

BALANCE OUT OF CHAOS

Rose Marie Novotny

ROSE MARIE NOVOTNY, M.A.

Copyright © 1988
Nature's Greening Press

First Printing
June 1988

Reproduction in whole or part, in any form,
including storage in memory device system, is
forbidden without written permission...except
that portions may be used in broadcast   or
printed commentary or review when attributed
fully to author and publication by names.

ISBN 0-9618982-2-4

LIBRARY OF CONGRESS CATALOG
CARD NUMBER: 88 - 90590

Inquiries or orders should be addressed to:

Nature's Greening Press
2322 Elliot Ave. So.
Minneapolis, MN 55404
612/870-9513

TABLE OF CONTENTS

CHAPTER   **PAGE**

ALSO WRITTEN BY THE AUTHOR:

TRAVELING ALONE
FOR FUN AND PLEASURE

RESOURCES FOR THE PERSON ALONE

PUBLISHED BY:

NATURE'S GREENING PRESS
2322 ELLIOT AVE. SO.
MINNEAPOLIS, MN 55404

CREATIVITY

TAKES   FLIGHT

BALANCE OUT OF CHAOS

ROSE MARIE NOVOTNY, M.A.

DEDICATED
WITH GRATITUDE
TO MY SISTER

VERONICA
NOVOTNY

WELCOME

CREATIVITY TAKES FLIGHT is based on the premise that everyone is creative, and deserves encouragement to use that creativity. It recognizes that sometimes creative work is not borne cheaply and may exact a price in pain and suffering. Likewise, the latter often ignites and enhances the creative spirit. Whatever avenue your creative expression takes, it unifies and balances all dimensions of life.

Though the creative spirit has limitless possibilities, yet we are faced with choices daily. Despite current thinking which says, "You can have it all," **in choosing everything, we really end up with nothing.** This book's subtitle, **Balance Out of Chaos**, describes the tightrope we often walk while juggling new and old thought patterns, relationships, or material possessions. Time-tested keys for maintaining that balance are shared.

In struggling with the creative process, I tend to agree with Mary C. Richards who said, **"We have to realize that a creative being lives within ourselves ... and we must get out of its way, for it will give us no peace until we do."**

Read -- and cherish your life.

May 1, 1988   Rose Marie Novotny
Minneapolis, MN

You have
resources
within
you
to resolve
every problem.

1.

CREATIVITY FOR EVERY AGE

The potential for creativity is present, to some degree, in every human personality. Though you may believe you're not creative, you were born with unique gifts of creativity. Unfortunately, many of society's systems, in an effort toward conformity and control, stifle creativity. Your family, school, church, work environment, government, or other organizations can discourage creativity so much, you eventually assume the belief you're not creative.

It takes a solid foundation of self-esteem and confidence for creativity, the power of expression, to grow. If these are lacking, and you sincerely believe you can do nothing to change matters, then your creativity is temporarily blocked. You cannot compose a symphony or a poem, design an architectural structure, knit a sweater, develop a hiking trail for a state park, or invent a cruise missile unless you think it's possible. **Until you believe in yourself and the creative process, you probably won't achieve what you have in mind.**

Some examples:

Until recently, most of us accepted hunger in the world as a reality, assuming that, regardless of what is done, hunger and poverty will always be with us. Within the last ten years, however, groups like The Hunger Project, Bread for the World, and Loaves and Fishes have organized in affirming and believing that **there can be an end to hunger in the world by the year 2000.**

Likewise, hundreds of new groups coming into existence are asserting that, because of the potential for mass destruction from nuclear weapons, **war is outdated and must be avoided.** However, we first need to imagine our own lives and that of our families in a peaceful world before it can happen.

Though President Reagan seemed to give credit only to the world leaders and their negotiators, it was also ordinary citizens of the world who work for peace, who brought about the INF treaty banning all medium and short range missiles, signed on that historic day,

December 8, 1987. All peace workers who believed this step was possible helped create it.

Many people are pessimistic about the future of the world. You may be too ~~ if you allow negativity in your life to block creativity and you fall into a victim mode. When you permit simple, not necessarily sophisticated nor expensive, creativity to fully blossom, the need for turmoil and violence decreases.

Trusting yourself, your feelings, and what's good for you, is part of the creative process. **If you allow free expression to grow, you'll be amazed at where it will lead.** Creating is an exhilarating and energizing experience with its own momentum, but it can be frightening to those who have learned mistrust. It seems you either create or destroy, for **"Man deprived of his power of expression expresses himself in a drive for power."** (Jose Arguelles) The person devoid of creative expression who refuses, or is unable, to deal with his or her chaotic life, often spreads destruction on those around, simply by his or her physical presence.

Underdeveloped creativity is related to high unemployment, the farm crisis, acid rain, terrorist attacks, the county's welfare rate, teenage suicide, and mental illness. Upon reflection, you discover it touches **everything**, including the topsoil blown from Minnesota farmlands, which may now be a part of soil in Iran, and forgetting that **you contain at least one molecule from the dust of the original star.** Instead of using ingenuity for death-dealing weapons and destruction, the best scientific minds could be encouraged to use their gifts toward developing meaningful jobs, a more just economy, and the arts. **Nurturing creativity, the future of the world is brighter and more hopeful.**

What enhances creativity?

- Time and space to think.
- Beauty of nature.
- Desire for creativity.
- Focusing, concentration, and perseverance.
- Not dulling the mind with excessive TV, drugs, food, etc.
- Encouraging dreams.
- Pain and suffering worked through. (See chapters 2 & 3)
- A healthy lifestyle including physical activity.
- Being around creative persons.

An example of the creative process was the writing and publishing of my first book, **TRAVELING ALONE FOR FUN AND PLEASURE.** After allowing myself to become paralyzed by instructions that it should be done in a certain way, I reclaimed my own power and did it in a way which suited my style. With the help of my Macintosh computer, I not only wrote it, but edited, designed, illustrated, and published the book. My creativity had been frozen by my need for perfection and the fear of success. When I let go of perfectionism and enjoyed small successes, creativity was released.

Creative work delights, affirms, and sparks others' creativity. As other people see what you've accomplished, they say, "Why, if you did that, then maybe I can do _____. I've always wanted to do that." After reading **TRAVELING ALONE**, people told me they've taken trips, published some of their own work, or had courage to do what needed to be done, all adding meaning to this effort.

● ● ● ● ● ● ● ●

You may choose to allow others to squash and squelch your creativity. But when supportive and nurturing people say, "**Yes, you can do it**," you can learn to believe that, too. Creativity doesn't have to be a major production. Perhaps it's something very small, but if it's important to you, it's worth going after.

You have resources within you to resolve every problem. The human mind and its ability to cope with, adjust to, and create anew is fantastic and unlimited. As you allow your vision to expand and you trust your own giftedness, nothing can stop you from realizing your fondest dreams.

SUGGESTED READING

1. Fox, Matthew. A SPIRITUALITY NAMED COMPASSION. Bear and Company, Santa Fe, NM: 1984.
2. Ueland, Brenda. IF YOU WANT TO WRITE. The Schubert Club, St. Paul, MN: 1984.

NOTES AND REFLECTION

1. What are the circumstances when you feel most creative?

2. What are your favorite forms of creativity?

3. Allowing yourself no barriers, make a list of all the creative things you'd like to do in your lifetime.

4. Star the most important items on the list. How can you achieve them?

TRANSITION:
LIFE DISINTEGRATION

The journey of life takes you through many passages, and the older you are, the more frequently they seem to occur. Some of these passages are crises when life seems to fall apart around you. **When your life falls to pieces, you feel complete confusion as you seem to plummet through space.** When disintegration and destruction take place inside or out, there's nothing to hang onto. Simply stated, if you choose to grow, you have to let go of the old to embrace the new, much easier said than done.

In the fall of 1978, I moved to Chicago to do graduate work at the Chicago Theological Consortium. I chose a particular school, the Jesuit School of Theology Chicago, for its emphasis on justice and ministry. But the studies reflected my withered spirit and seemed irrelevant and impractical.

The upheaval which began theologically and continued emotionally would eventually encompass all areas of my life. It lasted through both years of study, the first at JSTC and the second at Mundelein College, and returned with me to Minnesota for two more years before its resolution. The move to Chicago both symbolized and provided the setting for the breakup, described in the next two chapters, to occur.

This story of disintegration and transition is roots for CREATIVITY TAKES FLIGHT. The latter, in turn, is rooted in a spirituality of creation (see chapter 4).

It had been
a journey
into the unknown~~
giving meaning
to what
had gone before,
and courage
for what was
yet to come.

2.

CHICAGO 'N LONELINESS

Life in Chicago, with its population of over six million people, was challenging and difficult. Day-to-day struggles left little energy for developing caring relationships. Though I saw overabundance and overstimulation in many areas, compassion seemed limited. I saw many people living precariously on the edge of existence, dependent on properly working systems. When one part of a system broke down, like the elevated trains, a large segment of the population was immediately in turmoil.

Chicago's worst winter of the century occurred in 1979-80 while I was attending graduate school. Returning there in January 1980, after Christmas holiday in Minnesota, a Chicago blizzard stranded me at the Minneapolis-St. Paul International Airport. Flights to and through Chicago's O'Hare Airport were cancelled and rerouted because of the storm. I finally caught a flight, getting the last seat on the plane, about eighteen hours later than my originally scheduled flight.

After I arrived in Chicago, I found my luggage buried in a mountain of suitcases, boxes, valises, and other containers, all of which were heaped together near the O'Hare Airport baggage carousels. Finding mine seemed short of miraculous, especially when I later heard about others who waited weeks for their misplaced bags.

The shuttle bus ride from the airport on the expressway and through the streets of Chicago was worse than usual. Then, while pulling my suitcase along icy streets and unshoveled sidewalks, I slipped and had a nasty fall, injuring my pelvis.

The street on the north side of our Chicago block in Hyde Park was never plowed from November until the snow melted toward the end of March. Also, "snowbirds," cars covered with snow, weren't towed. Apparently, city officials had no idea how to handle a major storm. Mayor Bilandic's inept handling of the situation was partially responsible for his ultimate loss of the next election as a disgruntled populace voted for a stronger leader.

The worst story I heard was that of a snowplow driver who had worked for several days without relief, and simply went crazy. His vehicle was stalled with many others in an expressway traffic jam. Exasperated, he drove his truck right over the cars behind and in front of him, killing one person and injuring several others.

For many weeks afterward, we heard horror stories of the suffering endured by the homeless, the poor, and deprived persons, many of whom were exploited by opportunists who took advantage of the misery created by the storm. Though I had lived through many harsh Minnesota winters, where storms frequently brought out cooperation and inventiveness in people, I'd never known one as wretched as the 1980 Chicago blizzard. It was hard keeping a sense of humor when life was in danger.

Because of it's size, unusual events occur in Chicago. The visit of Pope John Paul II in the fall of 1979 sent the city into a frenzy of preparations and extravagant spending. With the Pope's concern for the poor and homeless, it seemed that the millions of dollars spent could have been used more appropriately in their favor. I recall talking with a jaundice-eyed, runny-nosed, street person who wished he could've sold a few of the flowers at the papal Mass in Grant Park, and used the money for soup.

Surrounded by the Windy City's steel skyscrapers, miles of concrete, and desolate masses of people, I had rarely felt such intense loneliness. Along with my studies, I wanted to do something to alleviate the poverty I saw. **The alienation and desperation of the city's poor were touching my own experience, and my body felt like one gaping wound.**

Motivated to respond to the needs of the poor (myself included), I chose to volunteer to work with a variety of organizations. One was the United Farm Workers, who were supporting a boycott of Red Coach brand lettuce. Activities primarily consisted of distributing pamphlets and "billboarding," which meant standing on heavily trafficked streetcorners holding portable billboards inviting motorists to support the boycott. Since we wanted to attract the most visibility during morning and evening rush hours, we chose to rise early and stand in the darkness, snow and cold.

Responses we received included friendly honks, waves, and smiles of support as well as angry shouts, obscene gestures, and raised fists of derision. Our efforts, however, seemed worthwhile to us. We were helping achieve higher wages and better working conditions for impoverished farm workers, many of whom were undocumented migrants struggling to raise families.

A gratifying experience with this UFW group was organizing a fund-raiser at Mundelein College. Cesar Chavez, head of the UFW and a charismatic man, personally thanked each of us for our efforts.

Another cause I adopted was the Pontiac Prisoners Support Group, formed to support seventeen Black and Chicano prisoners in the Pontiac Prison. Overcrowded cells and atrocious conditions led to a prison uprising and the deaths of two guards. We attended some of the men's trials, wrote letters on their behalf, and shared their stories in a Prison Reform Forum. **We saw the connections between living conditions, lifelong unemployment and lovelessness, and poverty into which people were born, and the violence they then inflicted on others.**

Working with the National Association of Religious Women provided another avenue for my involvement. NARW championed women's issues through newslettters, boycotts, demonstrations, meetings, and marches on local and national levels. When I eventually returned to Minnesota, I continued working with the Chicago national office of NARW, but on a regional level within Minnesota.

All of this is not to say that my life was totally bleak, for there were times of happiness and laughter with gentle people who shared my days. **But the predominant feeling and memory of those years are a cold, gray, wintry day, and a small skiff abandoned upon a storm-tossed Lake Michigan.**

For my second year in Chicago, I transferred to the Institute for Creation-Centered Spirituality at Mundelein College on the north side. The program was imaginative and refreshing, and I thrived amidst creative persons from around the world. Since some of us had specialized interests, Matthew Fox, the director, encouraged us to develop courses beyond the prescribed. I enjoyed following my intuitions, and created a course of studies that suited my particular talents and needs.

Intellectually, my year was the most stimulating of my life, but emotionally, it too had its grief. That fall, my father lay on his deathbed in Minnesota. Though he blessed my return to my studies, I grieved his dying and death which occurred in late November. My disintegration continued.

At the end of the year, we had the option of designing a final project using any art form. I desired something special to integrate and complete the master's degree. Responding to my plea, my sister, Veronica, came from Minnesota to help me evaluate various possibilities.

We were soon inspired as we walked along the shores of Lake Michigan. The project we envisioned included original poetry, music, song, mime, and dance, based on my work and studies. Filled with encouragement Veronica gave me, I immersed myself in creativity which now flowed freely. My project completed, I presented it to ICCS director, Matthew Fox, and to several groups, who received it favorably. The learnings Chicago had to teach me were finished.

Life in Chicago

had forced changes
which I would never
 have confronted
 elsewhere
in other circumstances.

Taking the risks
 which presented themselves
gave me
 a unique opportunity.

It had been
 a journey
 into the unknown
giving meaning
 to what had gone before,
and courage
 for what was yet to come.

I returned ~~
 from what felt
 like a foreign country ~~
to my homeland
 in Minnesota,
unaware
 of the transition
 deepening within me.

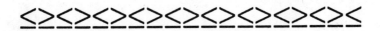

SUGGESTED READING

1. McGinnis, James. BREAD & JUSTICE. Paulist Press, New York: 1981.
2. Schaef, Ann Wilson. WOMEN'S REALITY. Harper & Row, New York: 1986.

NOTES AND REFLECTION

1. Describe some inner or outer journeys which changed your life.

2. What issues do you feel strongly about? Have you taken a stand on any? If so, describe them.

Aware of
what I gave up,
I did so
that I might
be open
to the new.

3.

BECOMING A NEW WOMAN

**REFLECTIONS ON
LEAVING RELIGIOUS LIFE**

After being a Roman Catholic Sister for twenty-five years, the time came for me to move on. The decision seemed to have made itself and was fully blossomed before I realized it. Facing reality and beginning the process of letting-go was hard work. Like my friends in marriages which had ended, the decision to change the course of my life was difficult. Though I chose not to see it coming because of its consequences, others around me later said they saw the evidence years before.

As I look back, the process began about five years earlier. I had a sense of restlessness, a dis-ease, like I no longer "fit" where I was and wanted to be part of a larger world. Thinking that more study was what I needed, I went away to graduate school. Two years' study was opportunity for growth but, returning home, the disconnection felt greater. Various measures, including different work, moving to a new home, and a major surgery, didn't remedy my dilemma. My life continued to disintegrate.

One day during the summer of 1982, I was talking with the director of Transition, a Twin Cities support network of former priests and sisters designed to aid in their adjustment to changed lifestyles. As I chatted with him that day, his simple statement, "You've already left," stunned me. I asked him to repeat his observation, and as his words penetrated my shield of denial, I recognized that this was what I was running away from.

I began therapy with a woman psychologist who was wife, mother, and former religious. What I thought would be short-term, turned into a long commitment toward wellness as I struggled with integration and many decisions created by life's new designs.

The first item on my list of priorities was finding a living space of my own. An open, airy, and comfortable third floor apartment in an older home in south Minneapolis, gave me the room I needed. Shortly after settling in, I invited the community director, the prioress, for dinner to inform her of my questioning process. Fortunately, she was an understanding and compassionate woman and I could share openly with her. Visibly saddened by my news, she affirmed and recognized the contributions I made to the community while a member. I was moved by her support when she encouraged me to do what I needed.

Telling the news to important people in my life was a difficult task. It took great courage to tell my older sister, also a member of the community, that I was leaving, but again, I was fortunate when she assured me of a continuing relationship, professional as well as personal.

Over the next few months, I met with significant people, to share my struggle and the change I was about to make. I had been advised and requested a Leave of Absence, a time of separation from the community similar to the separation which married couples frequently experience before divorce. It was a time to look at all aspects of my decision while still having a lifeline back, should I decide to remain. I initiated a name change, returning to my given name of Rose Marie from my religious name of Magdalen, or Maggie, as I was commonly called.

Before my leave of absence was announced, I wrote a letter to the community so the members would receive word from me directly. I had shared my daily life with many women whom I loved, and I cared about the way in which they heard the news. My preference would have been to tell each one individually, but that was not possible. **It was a painful time for them and for me, but separation anxiety was alleviated by openness and acceptance.**

Financial insecurity was a factor which prevented me, for a long time, from looking at leaving. I was temporarily employed by a major corporation, and was frightened about the future. But I knew what I needed to do, and trusted that all would work out for me. I asked for and received a thousand dollar loan from the community and, being a resourceful woman, was able to make that stretch a long way. However, without the inheritance which my parents left me at the time of their death, I would have fared poorly.

The teenager in me was activated by the prospect of owning my first "very own car" at age 45! Insecure about spending a lot of money, I invited my cousin, Milo, to join me shopping for one. I remember well that freezing January Saturday afternoon when we stepped into the car to go home after a fruitless search. A man he recognized pulled up next to ours. "You wouldn't know anyone who's looking for a good used car, would you?" the fellow inquired. "We sure do," replied my cousin, and we took the car for a test drive. It was the car I was looking for, and I bought it. I was thrilled with that handsome Plymouth Horizon, until my prized possession was totaled by a hit-and-run driver eighteen months later.

Though I had been advised by the director not to date during this time, I did, since exploring relationships with men was one of the reasons I wanted to change my committment. I knew men, including priests, with whom I had both good and unhealthy relationships. I longed for physical intimacy and wanted to be honest in expressing it.

Dating, after so many years of its absence, had both its funny and trying aspects. One of the humorous experiences was answering the personals ads and placing my own in the local "Twin Cities Reader." I received a variety of responses to mine, which read, "Fun-loving Marion seeks outdoor-minded Robin Hood for committed relationship in Sherwood Forest...."

I still laugh when I remember calling to meet five of the respondents whose letters indicated common interests. Though the letters made good reading, I discovered how different they were from the individuals, and after a first date, neither they nor I were motivated for more.

For nine months following leaving the community, I dated a twice-divorced man and discovered myself repeating destructive behavior patterns of unresolved issues with men. At the time of the car accident, the man I was dating left our relationship, and since then, my values and interests have changed. **Though some of my experiences now seem naive, I did grow through them.**

Six months following my leave, I took an exhilarating twelve day camping trip alone, circling Lake Superior. I recall driving from Thunder Bay, Ontario, to Grand Portage, Minnesota, on a brilliant Sunday morning. "It's time to ask for the dispensation," flashed through my mind, and I realized I was ready to complete my leave-taking. This meant informing the community director and writing a letter to the Sacred Congregation of Religious in Rome applying for the dispensation, a formal document signifying release from vows. **Because I valued myself and my past, it was important to fulfill all legal requirements.**

All went well. The dispensation arrived about six weeks later, and I carefully considered how to sign it. To witness the occasion, equally important to my entering the community, I chose my sister and a good community friend. Accompanying me that evening was a bottle of champagne and my camera. Afterwards, I attended a party with close friends. Several weeks later, my community friends hosted a farewell luncheon and transition party. **Having celebrated a job well done, and accomplished a satisfying closure, I was ready to move on.**

MAJOR CHANGES

When I look back at this major transition, the hardest part of it was not the actual leaving, but making the decision to do so. I felt guilt in giving up a commitment which I had intended to be for a lifetime. Not recognizing the signs of disintegration, I experienced pain, confusion, and anger. Once I made my decision, however, everything began falling into place.

Among the changes occurring was dissipation of my anger. For five years prior to my leaving, I was a militant feminist and social activist. I now sense the anger behind the militancy was toward myself for not being able to face what I needed to do. Not knowing where it originated, I was projecting it onto men. Hostility disappeared with making my decision, and my style of feminism now includes gentleness, sensitivity, and a sense of humor.

My relationship with the Catholic Church also changed. I am now less active in church affairs as I sadly watch women's gifts in leadership and decision-making unaccepted. My background in creation spirituality is a source of strength and support, and I trust my informal spiritual network while finding different ways to celebrate God's presence in the world. The goodness of a Higher Power has never been more clear.

My attitude toward money is a third change for me. Because I had taken the vow of poverty, and had little money to use, I saw it as unhealthy and "the root of all evil." Re-education in financial matters helped me see that **I deserve to enjoy the good things of creation,** and I am free of the guilt I once experienced. Though I continue to live a simple lifestyle and do not spend money frivolously, I enjoy the material things it can buy: dining out, a good car, better clothes, travels to foreign countries, and sharing it with others by supporting important projects.

Friendships also underwent an evolution. As I changed, so did my relationships. Women remain my closest friends.

My attitude toward work is different and I have let go of my need for overwork. **I earn an income in a variety of ways, knowing that who I am and what I bring to my work is as important as what I do.**

SOME QUESTIONS

Over the years, I've asked myself, "Would I do it again? Would I become a Sister again?" Knowing what I know about the world now, probably not; but knowing what I knew back then, I probably would. The options for women in the fifties were few if one did not choose marriage. Religious life for women was at its peak then, and though the discipline was rigid and strict, yet women in other walks of life also experienced restrictions.

Do I have any regrets about having lived that life? No. None. I lived it as fully as I knew how, with the knowledge that grew over the years. I took advantage of opportunities for growth which came my way, and was able to do many things I wanted. **It was not a perfect life, by any means, but it suited me at the time.** When I compared notes with my women high school classmates at my 30th year reunion, I realized I had done more and been more places than most of them had. I look back with gratitude for all of the experiences which brought me to where I am.

What was rewarding about the sisterhood? Though I met sisters with whom I had little in common or who had stopped growing, I knew others who were gifted, well-educated, dynamic, and extraordinary women. Looking back at the hundreds I knew from around the world, I realized how much I benefitted from having met them and that a part of them would always be with me.

Regarding my decision to leave, would I do it again? Yes, it was time for me to go. I was at a different stage in development and ready to make a new commitment to life. I assessed my original motives for becoming a Sister, and all had changed. My parents, an important though unconscious factor in my decision, were now dead.

Aware of what I gave up in choosing to leave, I did so that I might be open to new experiences. The curtain descended on a rich, meaningful drama of my life and rose on new paths for exploration.

SUGGESTED READING

1. Bridges, Wm. TRANSITIONS: MAKING SENSE OF LIFE'S CHANGES. Addison-Wesley, New York: 1980.
2. O'Collins, Gerald. THE SECOND JOURNEY: SPIRITUAL AWARENESS AND THE MID-LIFE CRISIS. Paulist Press, New York: 1978.

NOTES AND REFLECTION

1. What major transitions have you experienced?

2. Are aspects of it still unfinished for you?

3. What would it take to complete the transition?

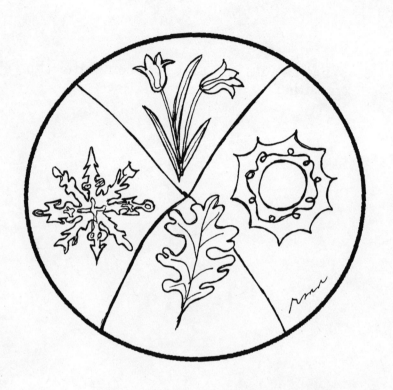

Creation
spirituality
affirms
that
the spiritual person
is always
in the right place
at the right time.

4.

A SPIRITUALITY OF CREATION

In the mid '70s, word again began spreading about "creation spirituality," a way of relating to God (or Higher Power) and the universe based on the goodness and blessings of creation. Instead of beginning with sin, as many traditions do, it begins with the human person as an **"original blessing."** This spirituality is as old as humankind, almost 15,000,000 years, but gradually became repressed after the Reformation.

Many of us were brought up in Christian church traditions which taught a theology of sin/fall/guilt and redemption. We were told that we were born with original sin which would always impact our lives, and that regardless of how hard we tried, we would always be imperfect beings, with a tendency towards evil. Furthermore, we were responsible, at least in part, for the death of Jesus. **This knowledge often made life burdensome and, though we tried very hard to do and be good, we never could measure up to the model presented.** We wanted to give up before we started.

As we learned about creation spirituality, however, we felt like we had "come home." Open to this new, yet very ancient, tradition, we wondered why it had taken so long to hear these basic, simple, and ordinary truths. For those of us weary of having others tell us what to do and what to believe, **it was refreshing to learn that creation spirituality welcomes utilizing personal responsibility and freeing creativity.** It respectfully accepts us as we are, without coercing change.

An understanding of creation spirituality can be approached from its **four paths** and **26 themes,** explained and developed in the book, **ORIGINAL BLESSING, written by Matthew Fox.**

The four paths are:

1. **Befriending creation.**
2. **Befriending pain, letting be and letting go.**
3. **The way of creativity.**
4. **A new creation of justice and compassion.**

Though we may feel that we are traversing one path exclusively at a particular time, generally we experience aspects of all four simultaneously.

The **first path** begins with the dawning of **creation**, with the belief that all that is created is good. It accepts human beings as original blessings being preeminently trustworthy, and sharing in the divinity of the Creator. **Themes** of this path include:

- Creation as blessing and enjoyment.
- Learning to trust.
- Panentheism (God is in us and we are in God).
- Realized eschatology (living in the present).
- The creative energy of God.
- A cosmic hospitality.

The **second path, befriending pain and darkness,** encompasses the four themes of letting pain be pain, letting go, and sinking into nothingness. It also recognizes sin as the refusal to let go, and the refusal to allow receptivity. It accepts pain as a healthy, integral, and unavoidable part of life, which, when faced and worked through, can lead to fullness and richness. (Examples of this path are detailed in chapters 2 and 3 of this book and in a forthcoming book on accidents and pain.)

The **path of creativity** emphasizes experiencing our creative side. Extrovert meditation is helpful in working through the dark times. As we sing, play, dance, rug hook, ski, bake homemade bread, wood carve, play guitar, etc., we experience ourselves as whole and well-balanced persons.

Several **themes** in this third path are:

- Being co-creators with the divine.
- Creativity as centering.
- Making our lives works of art and returning beauty to the world.

The **way of transformative justice, the final and fourth path**, realizes that our lives can be filled with compassion. Everything in the universe is interconnected and interrelated, and a part of everything else. (In fact, you may observe that all the chapters of this book, **CREATIVITY TAKES FLIGHT**, relate to one or other path and theme of creation spirituality.) Nothing that exists is unimportant or useless, and we are responsible to and for creation. **It affirms that the spiritual person is always in the right place at the right time.** Themes include:

- Creating a global civilization.
- A spirituality of the oppressed.
- God as mother and God as child.
- Compassion and celebration.

Much of the credit for dissemination of knowledge about creation spirituality in our time can be given to Matthew Fox, who founded the Institute of Creation-Centered Spirituality in Chicago. **The Institute of Culture and**

Creation Spirituality now resides in Oakland, California, where students come from around the world to study unique courses. The program now includes Psychology and Geo-Justice with Creation Spirituality, and Matthew Fox and others lecture to interested persons around the globe. The network in creation spirituality grows steadily as the good news spreads, and Creation Magazine, the organ of this network, writes of groups forming thoughout the world to share emerging spirituality. Gatherings include presentations on varied subjects and forms of artistic expression. The model for these groups is shared creativity and leadership rather than a hierarchical structure.

This spirituality, like any other tradition, has a family tree of writers and holy persons. Besides Matthew's many writings, these include little-known persons from the 12th to 14th centuries: Meister Eckhart, Hildegarde of Bingen, Mechtild of Magdeburg, Julian of Norwich, and Kabir. More recent persons making contributions to our understanding include Thomas Merton, Wendell Berry, Sigurd Olson, Frances Moore Lappe, May Sarton, Robert Bly, Susan Griffin, Meridel LeSueur, James Nelson, and others.

For many of us, knowledge of Creation Spirituality has made an important difference. Our love affair with nature, and much of what we innately believed from our earliest years, is validated. Primordial longing is affirmed, and we experience healing which comes when we are aware of the world's beauty. **Perhaps more than anything else, it allows us to blossom forth as "Original Blessings" with limitless possibilities for growth.**

SUGGESTED READING

1. CREATION MAGAZINE: Earthy spirituality for an evolving planet. P.O. Box 19216, Oakland, CA. 94619.
2. Fox, Matthew. ORIGINAL BLESSING. Bear & Company, Santa Fe, NM: 1983.
3. Nelson, James. EMBODIMENT. Augsburg Publishing, Minneapolis, MN: 1978.
4. Uhlein, Gabriele. MEDITATIONS WITH HILDEGARDE OF BINGEN. Bear & Company, Santa Fe, NM: 1983.

NOTES AND REFLECTION

1. How does creation spirituality relate to your understanding of the world?

2. As you grow in relationship to God and the creatures of the world, how is your life changing?

The playful child
in you
may be suppressed
for awhile,
but it awaits
being
awakened.

5.

PLAY-DOH™ AND ALL THAT STUFF

"I've never known anyone who could have fun like you do. You really know how to play!" are remarks you don't often hear as an adult. Images from childhood flash before you: youngsters spinning until they drop from dizziness, hanging upside down on the jungle gym, making sand castles, swinging gleefully, and walking around with paper bags over their heads. **Enjoying the present moment absorbed in carefree play is a rarer experience for adults.**

After many years of life programmed for work, you may not know the simple elements of play. As you give up control and let creativity emerge both inside and around you, you may even experience fear at its strangeness. All of creation, including humans, earth, sky, fire, and water, begin to look different.

Watching people's activities on holidays like Memorial Day, Labor Day, or Independence Day, you see a driven and desperate frenzy, instead of letting be and letting go, which play is about. The latter is more related to the pleasures of the natural world than to expensive toys or programmed and competitive sports.

For example, the **most pleasurable playtimes are frequently the least expensive**: walking around a lake or state park; sharing a meal and visit with a good friend; canoeing a quiet lake; watching a mother duck and her baby ducklings. Many times, *you don't have to do anything*. You simply have to be there and let it happen.

It's easy to lose sight of who you are, what you're doing here, and where you're going. But looking closely, you see evidence of what E. F. Schumacher suggests, that **the amount of leisure time you have is inverse to the amount of labor-saving devices you possess.** Rushing around to do the things which must be done may be an attempt to justify the nothingness you feel. Perhaps toys, gadgets, and appliances that simply must be bought are a cover-up for a feeling of emptiness inside.

How shocked people appear when you respond, "Playing," when they ask what you are currently doing. It's almost as though you had committed a serious crime.

Why it is difficult for adults to let go, to play and enjoy, may be due to:

§ Recriminations from childhood which taught you that "an idle mind is the devil's workshop."

§ Play not being valued in a production-conscious society, since no one told you (perhaps because they didn't know), that the playful mind is the creator's workshop.

§ The realization that nothing substantial is happening in life.

§ An inability to forgive.

§ Unresolved painful experiences which make you feel you're not good enough as you are.

Within you is a connection to all other beings in the universe, hungering for the development of your playful side. You can be stale, stiff, and stodgy only so long, and then your spirit begins to wilt. **But you can come alive again if you sing, dance, paint, rug-hook, garden, or do whatever your interest is. The playful child in you may be suppressed for a while, but it irresistibly awaits being reawakened.**

The playful child reminds me of the little girl I saw at a party one evening. As I watched her, I was fascinated by her total absorption in what she was doing, and the happiness which radiated from her as she played.

ÁÁÁÁÁÁÁÁÁÁÁÁÁÁÁÁ

Kari

Bouncing rubber ball of delight,
Your four years filled with
dancing and light.
Hopping on tip-toe,
Spinning the room with smiles bright.

Tire-less ~~
You seem to gain your energy
From folks who pat and nod
Affirming glances at artistry
held up with love.

ÁÁÁÁÁÁÁÁÁÁÁÁÁÁÁÁ

When your creativity is lost or stifled, you fail to see the options in life and tend to lose your sense of humor, and become sick or old before your time. **It's during relaxed playtime that you find lifesaving alternatives,** such as when you:

- sit in a patch of wildflowers and let them enliven you.
- walk slowly through an art gallery in the middle of the week and relish a favorite work of art.
- put a good record or compact disk on the stereo and shake loose the kinks in a weary body.
- borrow the kids' watercolors or color crayons and sketch a new scene.
- hug a new pink teddy bear.
- make a new fly for your fishing tackle.

Only you are responsible for the way you use your time. As co-creator in the universe, you can look for and enhance the playful side of creation as it expresses itself in the composition called LIFE. And when you know how to play, even the way you work changes.

SUGGESTED READING

1. Bly, Robert. THE KABIR BOOK. Beacon Press, Boston: 1977.
2. Novotny, Rose Marie. TRAVELING ALONE FOR FUN & PLEASURE. Nature's Greening Press, Minneapolis, MN: 1988.
3. Schumacher, E. F. SMALL IS BEAUTI- FUL. Harper and Row, New York: 1975.

NOTES AND REFLECTION

1. What are your most vivid recollections of play from childhood?

2. What are your favorite forms of play which encourage the child within you?

3. What kinds of play would you like doing but do not feel free to do?

4. What prevents you from doing the above?

"Up North"

Choose less
so that
you
might have more ~~
more enjoyment
of life
than before.

6.

A CHANGING WORLD OF WORK

As you consider the topic of creativity, one broad area for reflection is work life. You may be a person questioning the kind of job you have or the work you do because it seems to interfere with your creative life. If so, you are in good company with many others like yourself.

Assumed that it is good for the workers, a forty-hour work-week is the norm for many Americans. **Millions of people spend their work life following a Pied Piper who may lead them, not to the enchanted land they seek, but instead, to an arid desert.** Employees, lacking energy to seek alternatives and preferring not to make waves or exercise leadership, squirm to fit the mold. A few, identified with their work, would die if something happened to their jobs and they sometimes do.

Some people can work a 70-80 hour week and be no worse for wear. Other workers experience exhaustion and fatigue after 20 hours or less. Capacities vary and this must be taken into account.

Factors affecting work are:

- personal fulfillment (or not) found in work.
- energy level.
- health and age.
- emotional wellness.
- your attitude and philosophy regarding work.
- work motives and plans for spending money earned.
- self-esteem.
- preferences for doing other things with time.
- work history and its "success" and "failure."

There comes a point when what you are doing and the possessions you may have dictate your life. You may no longer be capable of deciding how to live, but something or someone else decides for you. **You are not living life; it is living you.**

Along with thousands of others, you start questioning the "rat race" mentality, quit your job which affords financial security, and search for satisfaction elsewhere. Perhaps you choose less so that you might have more ~~ more enjoyment of life than before.

Making the decision to work parttime or to quit a secure job is not easy. You may look back at what you've accomplished, see that is is useless, and feel empty. As you look to the future, the frustration that the "40 hours" does not create the hoped-for magic makes it evident that change is needed.

The mushrooming of temporary employment agencies and self-employment has many causes, including the one that workers want more options. Being a temporaries worker, you can choose a variety of work and flexible hours. It is a way of earning a livelihood ~~ satisfying though perhaps not wealth-producing ~~ while keeping your life intact. You can work for a time, pursue other goals, then work again. If a job is boring or the employer overbearing, you have the freedom to quit. The "temps" worker enjoys a natural kind of rhythm, attuned to the inner spirit.

I've worked "Temps" jobs for over five years. It began when I was unable to find a fulltime job I wanted. I accepted temporary positions to earn an income, and since, found that I enjoy working parttime and that I could make it financially doing so. In fact, it's

Temps work which often supports my creativity and allows me time for whatever I find alluring. I suspect I will want to continue working only parttime because it enhances my ability to live a normal life.

Perhaps you cannot remember not working. You've worked hard all your life, resulting in stress, burn-out, or illness. **Recovery from over-work and learning how to take better care of yourself may be a long process.**

A job may validate that you have a right to be here. However, work is not necessarily better than leisure and play. It is not a case of one or the other, for both are important and have separate roles. The key here is balance: **life in balance.**

People I know have made career changes so that they may live a more harmonious life. These include the doctor and single parent who decreased her work hours to spend more time with her two young sons; the chaplain, drained by years of giving, who resigned her position; the young man from a large corporation now stocking shelves in a food coop and moving furniture to pursue his dream of writing; the registered nurse quitting her job at the hospital who volunteered with First Call for Help. All are happier having made the decision to take more time for what they consider valuable, having reclaimed power over their own lives.

Though it may take some creative juggling, new ways of looking at work, and stepping into the unknown, it is possible to earn a salary to maintain a healthy and creative lifestyle, and still not miss the music to the dance.

SUGGESTED READING

1. Berry, Wendell. THE UNSETTLING OF AMERICA: CULTURE AND AGRICULTURE. Avon Books, New York: 1977.
2. Ferguson, Marilyn. AQUARIAN CONSPIRACY. J.P. Tarcher, Los Angeles: 1981.

NOTES AND REFLECTION

1. How do you feel about your work?

2. What are the positives and the negatives of your job?

3. Do you have a sense of any changes emerging for you regarding work?

4. Is it worth it for you to make any trades or exchanges for a more satisfying and healthy life?

5. What are you passing on to future generations with your work?

Perhaps
more than
anything else,
hospitality
speaks
of an
inner space
within.

7.

HOSPITALITY'S NOT OUTDATED

Do you ever wonder about the lost art of
hospitality, the kind which is only partially
involved with food and drink, but through
which you also come home satisfied? It's an
experience which gives you a good feeling all
over, because you are able to share a deep part
of yourself and someone truly hears and listens
to what and who you are. The good feeling also
comes from doing that for someone else: a
mutual enrichment. It's closely related to
"attention"--attending to, leaning towards--so
rare in this day of perpetual distraction that it
takes your breath away when you experience it.

The history of this piece dates back to the early fifties when TV was a new phenomenon. Perhaps you can recall being invited to neighbors' homes, and being compelled to sit in front of the tube whether or not you wanted to watch. TV watching with company is still habitual, and many homes have the box on constantly. Without searching for more creativity, some imaginations seem unable to move beyond a beer, Sunday afternoon sports, or a video movie.

Abraham Heschel once wrote:
"Home, inwardness, friendship, conversation are becoming obsolete.... We have no friends, we have business associates. Conversation is disappearing; watching television substitutes for the expression of ideas." (*The Insecurity of Freedom*, Schocken Books, 1975, p. 40.)

You may remember going home from a party or visit feeling awful, wishing you hadn't gone. There are all kinds of possibilities for this scenario: The host/ess doesn't really want to invite you in the first place but feels obligated out of duty, guilt, or ____(fill in with appropriate word). S/he talks on the phone for "hours" neglecting you to the point of extinction. The food is not ready so s/he escapes into the kitchen leaving the dog to entertain you, perhaps not so bad after all. The plumber is there fixing the sink, and you stand in the middle of the kitchen holding your coat for days.

Perhaps you have read accounts in the variety pages of the fabulous parties hosted by the rich and famous. But you don't have to be either to throw a good party--not necessarily a bash or a brawl--and to have a good time.

Some tips which work for satisfying entertaining include:

§ Gatherings for six to ten guests. When there are more than that, guests tend to get lost in the shuffle or get locked in the bathroom and no one knows they're missing.

§ Using cloth napkins and tablecloth, real dishes and silver instead of paper or plastic, and simple decorations. These increase value and celebration, something often lacking in our throwaway society.

§ **Being ready for guests when they arrive.** Though a seemingly trivial detail, if the host/ess is not ready, the guests may feel uncomfortable and unwelcome.

§ Preparing part of the meal yourself and then buying a take-out main course from a restaurant is not financially prohibitive and relieves you of some of the work as host/ess. Sometimes it's fun to do the whole meal and allow the guests to come bearing just themselves, though many parties now are potluck when guests bring a part of the dinner.

Recently, I had the happy fortune of being at a dinner party rated "five star." The above elements were present and the hostess carefully introduced each guest to the group as s/he arrived and shared how she happened to know the person. This made connections for us and we reached an early comfort-zone without having to make a bee-line for the bar. It gave us the opportunity to meet and enjoy one another and to experience the magic which occurs when special folks get together. Pleasure and delight were evident and we were gifted with something unique.

Memorable entertaining which warms your heart long after you've gone home does not necessarily take place within a huge mansion filled with expensive furniture. It can take place on a limited budget in an ordinary setting.

One day, I spent an impromptu wintry afternoon visiting my niece and her young son. She chooses, and has the opportunity, to work inside the home to spend valued time with her long-awaited child. As we relished and enjoyed one another's company, we discussed the difference between what made residences "homes" and others which resembled "motels."

It seemed related to "a person" being the focal point, the centering and stabilizing factor for those who came and went, someone to tend the fire, not only of the hearth, but also of the human spirit. If there was no one to make this difference, the house had an emptiness about it and people were not made welcome. The house lacked hospitality and warmth, and creativity would not blossom there.

Perhaps more than anything else, hospitality speaks of an inner space within. If people's lives are so cluttered with hundreds of details and activities, you sense no space or place to come in. **But when the host/ess has taken the time to clear an opening within the self, to create the warmth and expansion which are important ingredients for hospitality, then you know beyond a doubt that you are valued and treasured beyond comparison.**

SUGGESTED READING

1. Heschel, Rabbi Abraham Joshua. THE INSECURITY OF FREEDOM. Schocken Books, New York: 1975.
2. Lappe, Frances Moore. DIET FOR A SMALL PLANET. Ballantine Books, New York: 1985.

NOTES AND REFLECTION

1. What stories come to mind when you think of great or not-so-great hospitality you experienced?

2. What kind of hospitality do you value as guest and as host/ess?

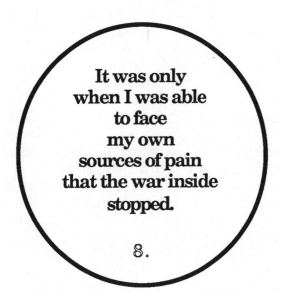

It was only
when I was able
to face
my own
sources of pain
that the war inside
stopped.

8.

NURTURING THE INNER PERSON

The year 1987, my fiftieth year of life, was a time for festive celebration. It was also natural for me to reflect on how I arrived at where I was, to assess some stepping-stones of my life and what nurtured me. What enabled me to grow spiritually and emotionally and gave me the care and support I needed?

Besides my obvious love for and nurturance from nature, several phases of my life emerged. One developmental stage took place in the mid-seventies when I worked in **adult education in large church settings.** Part of my job included organizing small groups for personal growth and shared prayer. Each met weekly and was comprised of from 25-30 members over the years, averaging about six participants. The meetings began with a discussion opener after which the group sharing moved on, with a life of its own.

I was inspired to see the women grow, blossom, and take charge of their lives, as dreams, hopes, and aspirations were strengthened by group support. Some who hadn't said a word for months gradually developed confidence to share. **What seemed impossible in isolation found courage to bloom amidst kindred spirits.** A close bond and natural networking occurred as the individuals shared openly and honestly. As some of us kept in touch over the years, we agreed this was a special time and place.

Several women from those support groups became lifelong friends. Somehow, when you've been in each others' lives for a while, pain inevitably becomes a part of the picture. And so, together, we've weathered death, divorce, illness, accidents, job change, depression, moves, and retirement. How fortunate we were to have had this bonding experience to see us through the hard times.

Another activity instrumental in my growth was **work in the peace and women's movements.** As board member of a variety of groups, I was involved in marches, demonstrations, meetings, lecturing, letter-writing, etc. Periodically, I stood back to see how my ideas grew, changed, and developed. I noted that the latter influenced how I used my time and energy for what I considered the greater good for the nation and world.

As I dealt with confrontation and violence, my experience and knowledge expanded. **Sometimes my own inner war matched the outer in which I was involved.** Looking back, I realize I desperately needed to "save the world," that is, myself, and chose to work it out in this fashion. My intent was to do what I could with what I had, wherever I was.

As I reflect, however, I find my words and works for peace were not always harmonious but sometimes added to the violence I was working against. It was only when I was able to face my own sources of pain that the war inside stopped, and my way of working for peace changed.

Living and working with politically and socially involved women was energizing as we worked toward common goals of changing what we saw as unjust systems. These experiences both empowered me and gave me opportunities for sharing that power with others. It was also exhausting since tremendous drive was required to accomplish our objectives.

An event for a period of two years in the early eighties which sustained me was a **monthly ritual gathering and potluck supper** we hosted at our home. Poems, readings, songs, dance, silence, shared food and stories drew us closer to one another. I looked forward to these gatherings for I knew I would receive strength and support in the creativity and exchange.

A lifetime value and constant source of nurturing has been **friendship relationships,** particularly those with women. I receive pleasure from some which go back to my earliest childhood days. Some of my richest moments occur when I talk with or see good friends, and I deliberately plan my schedule with this in mind.

When I spend time with warm, gentle, and caring persons, I receive a sense of physical and emotional well-being, and awaken the next morning filled with vitality. Friends are a special gift. Joy and satisfaction flow from sharing hospitality and stoking fires of friendship bonds which touched some passage of life. **Beauty from times like these, then, nurtures my inner woman and sparkles infinitely into the universe.**

SUGGESTED READING

1. LeSueur, Meridel. RITES OF ANCIENT RIPENING. Vanilla Press Inc., Minneapolis, MN: 1976.
2. Sarton, May. AT SEVENTY: A JOURNAL. W. W. Norton & Co., New York: 1984.

NOTES AND REFLECTION

1. What are some stepping-stones of your life? List approximately 12 entries to allow the significant ones to emerge.

2. What nurtures your inner self?

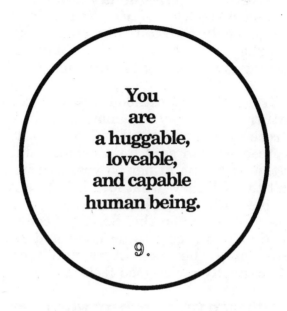

You
are
a huggable,
loveable,
and capable
human being.

9.

SELF-CARE WITH AFFIRMATIONS

Maybe in spite of yourself, you find yourself laughing when you hear a classic put-down from Lucy to Charlie Brown, from Johnny Carson or Joan Rivers. This "humor" is taken for granted and generously doled out at home, on TV, and in the marketplace. It may tickle you, but when it is aimed your way, the arrow may not feel so good.

It's wonderful if children grow up affirmed and encouraged. But many things said and done to children are not nurturing or supportive, and often children are raised in abusive and dysfunctional situations. **If you**

were given little support and encouragement while young, you frequently find it difficult to cope with stresses of life. Your vulnerable ego may be easily penetrated by sharp and caustic remarks or encased in a tough shell of "nothing is ever going to hurt me again."

Growing to adulthood without consistent nurturing, you may not know what it feels like to receive, much less how to give it. As a divorced woman said, in a caring relationship for the first time in her 65 years, "You know, I don't think I know what love is." **You need to receive positive strokes before you are able to give them.** When this has not been the case, you find it difficult to be open and receptive. Pain may be so ingrained that you automatically resist good feelings.

Although you were born with potential for creativity and a healthy dose of self-esteem, there may be times when you feel like people are just waiting to cut you down. People mean well, but their comments can be hurtful. Gradually your creativity suffocates and self-esteem shrivels, and your self-concept feels like the tinkling bell on the leg of a grasshopper.

Your self-concept can be described as the value judgment you place on yourself, or which others have put on you, which you accept as true. It can be your total composite of thoughts, feelings, and perceptions about yourself, based on life experience. The latter includes parents, teachers, church ministers, work managers and supervisors, friends and relatives, and the news media. All these feed data to your brain, which, not being able to distinguish between the good, bad, and the ugly, readily takes it in and soaks it up like a sponge.

A thoughtless remark said in passing can be devastating and play a vital role in your feeling worthless. Some examples:

- "You'll never amount to anything."
- "Boy, are you dumb!"
- "You are the ugliest kid I've ever seen."
- "Let's cancel the party because this baby girl is not the boy I wanted."
- "I think I'll trade you in for a newer model."

All comments you'd like to laugh at were they not so tragic. You need to learn how to cancel these to neutralize their impact.

Circumstances of life can deal you a stacked deck and add to or detract from your self-image. Being fired or not being able to find a job, becoming divorced, the death of a family member, drug abuse and eating disorders, an accident resulting in physical injury: all may affect the picture you have of yourself. The powerlessness and helplessness you feel, coupled with the guilt fanned by the complications of the situation can leave you feeling victimized.

You may view these happenings as personal failures and blame yourself for them. Your self-concept falls apart along with the disintegration of everything else. **If your foundation is shaky, even a simple non-event such as a casual remark can plunge you headlong into a chasm of self-destructive behavior.** You feel like you have to run constantly just to keep in place.

When your brain stores negative data from the past, taking responsibility for yourself is a difficult job. Burdened by this, you no longer believe in your own resources. You stop expecting good things and think you don't make a difference in the world. Experience teaches you not to look for any ripe blackberries on the bushes! **You learn that you do not get what you want, you get what you expect!**

What can you do about a diminished sense of self, to increase your possibilities for growth? To create a healthier self-image, a first step is a change in attitude and thinking. Positive thoughts create positive acts.

Negative thinking sets into motion negative actions. **You need to feed yourself a new diet of possibilities to counteract the unhealthy frame of mind and body into which you've fallen. Rather than waiting for others to shore up your sagging self, you can affirm, love, and take care of meeting your own needs.**

You can learn to love yourself and develop your own centering without waiting for the crumbs you may have expected in the handout line. Using personal affirmations, you can give yourself what you need, filling the empty part of yourself with self-love. **You turn around from hoping for "freebies," to becoming self-sufficient and fully employed as a whole person. From having an overdraft in your account, you now have sufficient funds to start writing checks.**

One way to counteract the destructiveness connected with poor self-image is doing a systematic and consistent self-affirmation program. **Affirmations verbally describe a desired condition, state, or thing, and can create what you want in your life.** They are read by the eye, said aloud or silently, listened to by the ear, and vividly pictured by the imagination.

I was first introduced to this process when I faced a major transition. Saying affirmations helped me achieve the things I wanted to do and become the person I wanted to become. Now a part of my daily routine, these little positive sayings enable me to make changes gradually and respectfully instead of suddenly and violently. As John Boyle stated, "There is no such thing as a human being. There are only human becomingnesses."

Affirmations were also useful after a serious car accident, when I needed to refocus my life with a new agenda. Some that were beneficial were:

- I like myself and I like loving myself.
- I am able to relax and let go every day.
- I am completely responsible for the way I respond to people and events.
- I replace a feeling of abandonment with self-confidence and empowerment.
- I open myself to the pain and let it energize my new work.
- I am a huggable, loveable, and capable person and I have a right to be here.

As months went by, I added other specific ones to my list. My restored health and energy can be attributed, in part, to my mental image of wellness (totally healed and cross-country skiing at Wild River State Park) as I said my affirmations.

If affirmations are said and imaged consistently, done with a believable hope in their achievement, and the affirmed item is deeply desired and for your good, they are effective and become reality. As William James said, **"Whatever the human mind can perceive and believe it can achieve."**

An example of such belief, confidence, planful problem solving, and tremendous determination was the 1986 Steger North Pole Expedition. The eight members of the group and their 49 dogs faced monumental odds in their thousand mile trek to their goal. But as Will Steger, co-leader of the expedition, remarked in the book recounting the adventure, **"The journey was proving to be a metaphor of life; goals are achieved by focusing on one step at a time."**

Perhaps you wait for tomorrow, next year or whenever to do the things important to you. Or, destined for disapointment and dependency, you wait for someone else to make your life better. **Living affirmatively, you can spend each day to its fullest capacity, as if there was no yesterday and will be no tomorrow, but only an eternal progression of nows.**

If you have been emotionally scarred by your past, you may need to do some personal work, including therapy and artistic expression, to help you deal with what continues to haunt you. With a variety of means, you are able to move beyond what constricts you, remember, and fly free. **You are a special and gifted person and the world awaits your unique contributions.**

If a seeming-tragedy occurs in your life, you can turn it around and have it work for you as a benefit and blessing. The Chinese character for the word *crisis* includes the idea of opportunity. You can use every experience, including the worst, as new opportunities for growth, expansion, and creative ways of living. You are a huggable, loveable, and capable human being, loved unconditionally by a greater power in the universe.

****

BASIC AFFIRMATIONS
TO BE SAID DAILY

1. I LIKE MYSELF AND I LIKE LOVING MYSELF.

2. I AM ABLE TO RELAX AND LET GO EVERY DAY.

3. I NEVER PUT MYSELF DOWN OR GIVE WAY TO DESTRUCTIVE BEHAVIOR.

4. I TREAT PEOPLE WARMLY AND RESPECTFULLY.

5. I AM COMPLETELY SELF-DIRECTED, GUIDED BY A HIGHER POWER, AND ALLOW OTHERS THE SAME RIGHT.

6. I TAKE TOTAL RESPONSIBILITY FOR THE WAY I RESPOND TO PEOPLE AND EVENTS.

ΩΩΩΩΩΩΩΩΩΩΩΩΩ

HOW TO CREATE AFFIRMATIONS

1. Make a list of all you want to achieve or become. For example:
   -I want to go to Alaska next year.
   -I'd like an Olds Ciera or a 4WD Jeep.
   -I want to improve my relationship with _____.
   -I want a Macintosh computer.
   -I'd like to live on the North Shore of Lake Superior for a year.

2. State precisely what it is you desire. For example:
   -I want a Macintosh computer system under $2500 from a computer store and sales rep I trust.
   -I'd like to live on the North Shore for a year in a secluded and safe cabin or house with pleasant surroundings, for under $xxx a month, within the next two years.

3. Now write each item on your list as a stated reality. Writing in the future tense often keeps the desired item out of reach. For example:
   -I love driving my new Cutlass Ciera and am able to manage the financing on it.
   -I am huggable, loveable, and capable and have a right to be here.
   -My two week vacation in Alaska is beautiful and I am warm, safe and healthy, and have good weather.

4. Do not put a time frame on the results. Life occurs at its own pace and schedule and when things are best for us.

5. After you've made your list of affirmations (between 5-8 when you first start and not more than 15 after it has become routine) say each one about 5 times upon rising or right before retiring. (It takes about 10 min.) Since change usually does not occur instantly, it may be months or even years before results take place. Sometimes, you may be pleasantly surprised by the affirmed item happening immediately. For example, the very day you begin affirming a new job, you get a phone call offering you one!!

6. Allow a pleasureable mental image or picture to accompany the affirmation as you say it. The more enjoyable the picture, the more readily will the mind absorb it: For example, while affirming a trip to Nova Scotia, let maps and pictures of it float through your imagination.

7. Because you grow and change and because old affirmations often become reality, you will want to drop the ones which no longer apply. It is recommended saying the Basic Six (above) daily, and perhaps writing other new ones at the beginning of each month. If an affirmation no longer feels appropriate or desireable, feel free to take it off your list.

8. At a time of crisis, write an emergency affirmation to deal with the situation. This can be said throughout the day or night as often as necessary until the situation is alleviated.

9. You may wish to tape record your affirmations with a musical background, but keep the program simple and manageable.

10. Close your eyes and enjoy a new and positive reality as you say your affirmations. Playing with them can give you a new perspective and a broader vision of what your life can become. **"Whatever is perceived and believed can be achieved."** (Wm. James)

ΩΩΩΩΩΩΩΩΩΩΩΩΩ

SUGGESTED READINGS

1. Briggs, Dorothy Corkille. CELEBRATE YOURSELF: MAKING LIFE WORK FOR YOU. Doubleday, New York: 1977.
2. EACH DAY A NEW BEGINNING. Hazelden Foundation, Center City, MN: 1982.
3. Steger, Will. NORTH TO THE POLE. Times Books, New York: 1987.

NOTES AND REFLECTION

1. Do # 1 above.

2. Do # 2 above.

3.   Do # 3 above.

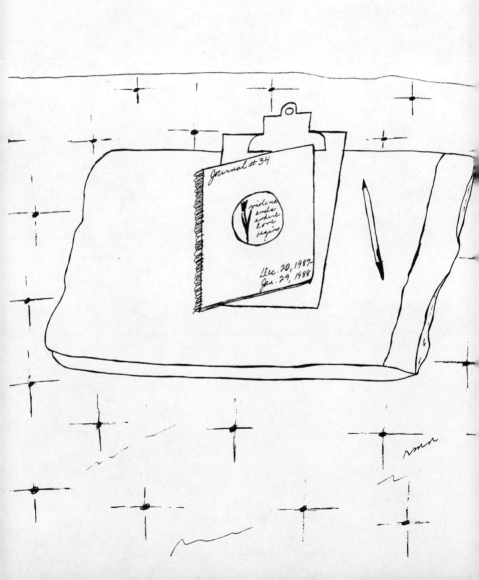

**Journaling
is a partner
in reality
and can help
keep you
grounded and
balanced.**

10.

MIRRORING THE JOURNEY: CONVERSATIONS WITH SELF

In a rushed and often frenzied society, the simple tool of journaling allows you to stop your life, to step back and examine it, put it in perspective, and do with it what you wish. If you are interested in getting to know yourself better and developing more of your resources and creativity, you can begin writing and keeping a journal.

Journaling helps you become more aware of what is going on and can bring to light an inner consciousness and harmony. **It develops**

and enhances creativity that you might not know you have, and helps you become an expert in your own life. This process prevents compartmentalizing life issues by surfacing the bigger picture. It is, however, only one aspect of healthy self-care. (Other dimensions include a healthy spirituality, living affirmatively and creatively, eating nourishing foods, and doing life-giving work and exercise.) Another helpful purpose for journaling is to provide closure for some of life's experiences. Many people never finish events and situations and leave details hanging, which creates dissatisfaction. If you are honest with yourself in the journaling process, you will experience closure naturally.

If you are driven by exterior demands, you may be unaware of allowing the creative process to draw you. Utilizing journal work can help you become attuned to your creative side and allow you to follow your dreams instead of persuasive advertising which deceives you. When you let the creative spirit have free rein, every day is a good day. You are no longer driven -- you are allured by creativity.

Though each person's style is unique, **journals often contain thoughts, feelings, perceptions, reflections, dreams, hopes, and aspirations.** Well-known journal writers come to mind: May Sarton, Sigurd Olson, Jessamyn West, Annie Dillard, Thoreau, and Edwin Teale. Though it may not be your intent to be published as they were, you can read how vital journaling was to each of them.

In DOUBLE DISCOVERY, Jessamyn West
writes of the lives of journal writers:

"Journal keeping is as necessary to
them as breathing. The life they live
is vaporous and unreal until
recorded in words in their
journals....They put down in ink
what they would never permit their
tongues to say." (p. 237)

**There are many ways to go about writing a
journal.** You may simply record your stream
of consciousness or thoughts. During times of
change and transition, you can write of the
upheaval, confusion, and turmoil going on in
your life and find anchorage in a quiet harbor.

Dreams are little hidden doors in the
innermost and secret recesses of the soul
opening into the cosmic night of self. Students
of dreams are able to learn about what was not
consciously available. You may keep a
separate dream journal or incorporate the
dreams along with other material, faithfully
recording them as you awaken.

Sometimes you converse or dialogue with
yourself, other persons, events, places, or
things, an exercise especially beneficial to the
single person, living alone. This helps sort-out
thoughts of what you may want to say to
another. Journals often contain letters written
to persons who are not presently available to
you, who may have died, and who may never
see the letter.

Nothing is off-limits to you, the writer, for the journal is where you can be most sincere and find the mirroring necessary in life. Your writing can be sloppy or neat, have misspelled or crossed-out words, and be ungrammatical. You may also illustrate your writing with drawings or paintings. **The important thing is the opportunity to express yourself.**

The journal can contain lists of many kinds (see "Lists" etc., pp. 103-110):

- "to do's;"
- pros and cons of a particular situation;
- the best events that have happened during the year;
- your goals for the new year;
- a list of gratitudes and good things;
- your affirmations (see chapter 9).

A journal can be written in daily or whenever you wish. There are periods when you may not write at all, while other times, you may write several times a day. **Journaling is a partner in reality and can help keep you grounded and balanced in a world of little security.** It has the advantage of gathering in one place a running commentary of your subjective experiences as you move through your life at a particular time.

Setting aside a specific time, whether it is every day or once a week on weekends, is especially important, for if you do not do this, your best intentions tend to get lost. Finding your own place and space to write is also vital.

It seems that when you have a "special place," you and your journal are attuned and writing flows more easily.

Your preference for writing instruments may include pens, sharpened lead pencils, computers and word processors, or typewriters. Notebooks from a stationery store, fancy hard-covered and bound books, legal yellow pads, and rolls of paper in an automatic printer may suit your needs at different times.

Re-reading the journal can be enlightening. You tend to forget painful, stressful, and unpleasant times in life when all is flowing smoothly and the sun smiles upon you. When you're in pain, you feel like you've been there for a thousand years and will never recover. Reading about a different period in life can encourage you that things are improvable.

At other times, you think that nothing is going on in life and yet, when you re-read your writing, you see the changes and growth taking place. **The evidence is in and you have written it.**

Re-reading your journal can help maintain the thread of continuity in your life. You will find more connections in your life if you re-read your preceding passage before beginning any new writing. Longer sessions can be done at year's end, after a specific period of life such as a birthday, if you want to assess a relationship or some event, or when you complete a notebook. **Re-reading your writing can be as fascinating as any gripping novel or tall tale.** Agreeing with Socrates that "The unreflected life is not worth living," you may wish to make observations if any synthesis has surfaced.

The journaling process is helpful in my life's work. I was introduced to it when I participated in several Ira Progoff "At a Journal Workshops," and have utilized the process ever since.

My favorite place to write is in bed, usually first thing in the morning and last thing at night. Some of my best journaling takes place at 2:00 or 4:00 a.m. when my creative side will not leave me in peace until I have switched on the light and written what is percolating within. I've been known to write in the middle of the night sitting in the bathroom in Jamaica, on the Nova Scotian shore of the Atlantic Ocean where some of this was written, in a canoe in the Boundary Waters Canoe Area in northern Minnesota, flying in an airplane, and sitting in a motel room.

Taking my journal with me is one way I keep my life focused wherever I am. **I frankly admit that I would be lost without this simple, inexpensive, and dependable tool which has proved so helpful,** for I would soon lose my inner balance were I deprived of it. It is as nourishing to me as fresh fruit and vegetables.

At the present time, I am writing my 35th journal, and have written over 5000 pages. Though some people like to save their journals, possibly for posterity, I choose to keep only the journals which pertain to my current life period. After I grow through certain experiences and closure occurs, burning the written pages and letting them return to the universe is a healthy and healing event. In another way, it says, "This is finished."

Any of the above exercises may be used with anyone who is able to write, including very young children and teenagers. In fact, many educators are now including this way of reflection in the learning process. In recent months, I have heard of senior high math and primary teachers using this effectively with their students.

When you take the time to record the thoughts which are most important to you at the time, your memories will always be there for you. They unfold joy and challenge of facing your own wildness, and birth a sense of oneness with the universe. You experience freedom, beauty, silence, companionship, empowerment, and fun. The feeling of fullness and creative completion you give to yourself through journaling need never end.

SUGGESTED READING

1. Progoff, Ira. AT A JOURNAL WORKSHOP. Dialogue House Library: New York, 1975.
2. Rainier, Tristine. THE NEW DIARY. J. P. Tarcher & Co., 1978.

NOTES AND REFLECTION

1. Do you write or have you ever kept a journal?

2. What was the experience like?

3. Is journaling important for you?

4. What thoughts would like to be written today?

ØØØØØØØØØØØØØØØØØØØØØØ

ΩΩΩΩΩΩΩΩΩΩΩΩΩ

May 1, 1988

Dear Reader:

Thank you for joining me on this flight into creativity. May your creative self venture into uncharted waters and places in the universe you've not known before.
Please note that the following pages include possibilities for "lists" of various kinds, should you be interested in using them.

If you wish to share thoughts or reflections with me, please contact me through:

NATURE'S GREENING PRESS
2322 Elliot Ave. So.
Minneapolis, MN 55404

Respectfully,

Rose Marie Novotny

Rose Marie Novotny

ΩΩΩΩΩΩΩΩΩΩΩΩΩ

Fill your life
with
THE GOOD,
THE TRUE,
AND THE BEAUTIFUL,

for in the end,
that is what
will flow
from you.

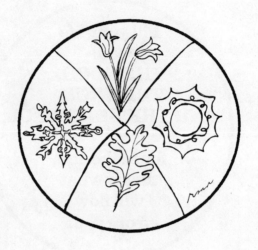

ΔΔΔΔΔΔΔΔΔΔΔΔΔΔ

About the author:

Rose Marie Novotny has been involved in education at some level since 1961. She holds degrees from the College of St. Catherine (B.A. Education) and Mundelein College, Chicago (M.A. Spirituality). Her first book was TRAVELING ALONE FOR FUN & PLEASURE, which will be followed by her third effort, ACCIDENTS & PAIN - What To Do If They Happen To You.

A creature of the universe, Rose Marie's heart is at home in Minnesota, her birthplace. She considers it the most wonderful place on earth to live, and currently enjoys a balanced and creative life in Minneapolis. Eventually, she hopes to follow her own heart's desire and move "Up North."

FAVORITE QUOTES

"TO DO" LIST

AFFIRMATIONS

DRAWINGS

BOOKS I WANT TO READ

GRATITUDES LIST

I am thankful for:

NOTES

THINGS I'D LIKE
TO ACCOMPLISH SOMEDAY

For those
who are able
to realize
how much
God loves them,
ALL THINGS
work together
unto good.

ORDER FORM

CREATIVITY TAKES FLIGHT:
_____copy (copies)
Enclose $6.57 plus $.43 Mpls, Mn. sales tax, and $1.00 for shipping & postage for each copy.
Total: $8.00.

TRAVELING ALONE FOR FUN AND PLEASURE:
_____copy (copies)
Enclose $2.82 plus $.18 sales tax, and $.80 for shipping of each copy.
Total: $3.80.

From:

Name_____

Street
Address_____

City, State
Zip   Code_____

Enclose check for correct amount and mail to:

**Nature's Greening Press
2322 Elliot Ave. So.
Minneapolis, MN 55404**